DAVIS

GW00598813

John Hayes (b 1945) grew up on the U.S. West Coast, and has spent much of his life camping and backpacking in Oregon's scenic Cascade Range. A native of Eugene, Oregon, he studied psychology at the University of Oregon, graduating in '66.

Mr Hayes first came to Nepal in the fall of 1969 on his way home from a three year assignment as a Peace Corps volunteer in South Thailand. His attachment to Nepal was quickly and solidly formed during a month long trek to the Everest region; he remained until the following spring, trekking extensively through East Nepal and the Central Terai, including Chitawan National Park.

After a three year interlude in the U.S. working in the field of Environmental Health, Mr. Hayes returned to Nepal in 1973, this time with his wife, Beverly, a travel agent in Oregon. They spent a full year trekking in the Thak Khola, Helambu-Langtang and the Solu-Khumbu regions, researching a series of three trekking guidebooks and a number of articles on trekking in Nepal.

Publisher's Note

The experience of trekking in Nepal may be used to enrich not merely a visit to this fascinating mountain kingdom, but indeed life itself, for to move about amongst the highest and most awe inspiring peaks on earth is truly memorable.

The Government of Nepal has organised trekking in an efficient and helpful way, working through a number of authorised licensee trekking agencies.

Porterage and planning are of a high standard, but persons participating in these treks will certainly benefit from study before and during these treks of the relevant trail guides.

As a result of feedback from trekkers in Nepal, we venture to add three comments to Mr. Hayes' trail guide.

First, litter on the trail can be of disturbing proportions. No true lover of mountains will gladly tolerate this and we express the hope that at least readers of this book will do what they can to leave lunch stops and camp sites in orderly condition. The out-door code suggests one should leave such sites 'as they were when you found them' — from all accounts there is scope on some treks to leave the sites in even **better** condition than they were when you arrived. Think of the people who will be following you.

Second is the question of timing. September is not always bad. There is an element of risk in the weather and views may not always be quite as good, but the trails are much less crowded and conditions can be that much more pleasant.

Third, don't go into the back country with currency notes of large denomination. Rather carry notes of low denominations together with plenty of coins. Change is not always easily come by and with bed or a meal for as little as 3 rupees it will pay to plan your cash-in-hand accordingly.

Trekking North of Pokhara

Jomsom, the Thak Kola Canyon and the Annapurna Sanctuary

by John L. Hayes

 Roger Lascelles, Cartographic and Travel Publisher
47 York Road, Brentford, Middlesex TW8 0QP Telephone: 01-847 0935

Publication Data

Title	Trekking North of Pokhara
Typeface	Phototypeset in Compugraphic Times
Photographs	The Author and where indicated, by Paul Morris
Printing	Kelso Graphics, Kelso, Scotland.
ISBN	0 903909 14 6
Edition	This fourth July, 1987
Publisher	Roger Lascelles
	47 York Road, Brentford, Middlesex, TW8 0QP.
Copyright	Avalok Publishers, Kathmandu

All rights reserved. Other than brief extracts for purposes of review no part of this publication may be produced in any form without the written consent of the publisher and copyright owner.

Distribution

Africa:	South Africa —	Faradawn, Box 17161, Hillbrow 2038
Americas:	Canada —	International Travel Maps & Books, P.O. Box 2290, Vancouver BC V6B 3W5.
	U.S.A. —	Hunter Publishing Inc, 155 Riverside Dr, New York NY 10024 (212) 595 8933
Asia:	Hong Kong —	The Book Society, G.P.O. Box 7804, Hong Kong 5-241901
	India —	English Book Store, 17-L Connaught Circus/P.O. Box 328, New Delhi 110 001
	Singapore —	Graham Brash Pte Ltd., 36-C Prinsep St.
Australasia	Australia —	Rex Publications, 413 Pacific Highway, Artarmon NSW 2064. 428 3566
	New Zealand —	Enquiries invited.
Europe:	Belgium —	Brussels - Peuples et Continents
	Germany —	Available through major booksellers with good foreign travel sections
	GB/Irleand —	Available through all booksellers with good foreign travel sections.
	Italy —	Libreria dell'Automobile, Milano
	Netherlands —	Nilsson & Lamm BV, Weesp
	Denmark —	Copenhagen - Arnold Busck, G.E.C. Gad, Boghallen, G.E.C. Gad
	Finland —	Helsinki — Akateeminen Kirjakauppa
	Norway —	Oslo - Arne Gimnes/J.G. Tanum
	Sweden —	Stockholm/Esselte, Akademi Bokhandel, Fritzes, Hedengrens. Gothenburg/Gumperts, Esselte Lund/Gleerupska
	Switzerland —	Basel/Bider: Berne/Atlas; Geneve/Artou; Lausanne/Artou: Zurich/Travel Bookshop

Contents

The new section on Dumre to Manang has been written by Stan Armington who has been trekking and organising treks in Nepal since 1969. He is currently Managing Director of Himalayan Journeys — a trekking company based in Kathmandu.

Preface

Thomas Cook & Sons Ltd, the travel agents, along with the legendary Boris Lissanevitch of Kathmandu, arranged for sixty people to disembark at Kathmandu, in the year 1955, as one of their stops in their tour itinerary. Of the sixty, the 5th of March 1955, saw twenty arrive at Tribhuwan Airport in a chartered aircraft, with the balance following on the 7th and 9th in groups of twenty. *These were the very first people who were officially permitted to come as tourists to, till then, mythical, mysterious and forbidden Nepal. The year 1974, saw Nepal host to close on ninety thousand tourists.

With this increase in people curious about our unique culture and history, our temples and handicrafts, there has been a corresponding mushrooming of people who have come to trek in our homeland. Our incredible topographical inheritance contains the lush ricefields and tropical jungles of the Terai, the gentle hills, valleys and forests of midland Nepal, the alpine meadows, yak pastures and frozen lakes of the lower Himalayas to the craggy summits of the most rugged range of mountains on earth, including Sagarmatha, the highest mountain in the world.

The aim of this trekking guide, which we have felt long overdue, is to give detailed guidance regarding the terrain, and all relevant information required, for one to be adequately prepared for the trek. For this could mean the difference between a trek with beauteous grandeur and revelations of Nature at her most magnificent and a sojourn, which besides being painful and cold, might be a most unhappy experience.

The serial number of this book, number two in a three title series at present, does not imply any grading of the treks it describes. They have been separated for the convenience of the majority who come and have time for only one trek. Ours is a country of the most enchanting beauty, and if any one book in this series helps you to enjoy an unforgettable experience, our efforts will be fully justified.

February 1976
Kathmandu

*Source: the original host at The Royal Hotel, Boris Lissanevitch, now — The Yak & Yeti.

Introduction

The region north of Pokhara along the southern slopes of the Annapurna Himal, and beyond Annapurna and Dhaulagiri in the Thak Khola canyon, offers what no other major trekking route can give; dramatic close-up views of some of the highest and most beautiful mountains in the world and a chance to penetrate through the Himalayan barrier into an arid inner Himalayan valley which, both culturally and geographically, has much in common with Tibet.

The abrupt variations in altitude found here are often astonishing to westerners who are accustomed to calling the Rocky Mountains high or the Snake River gorge deep; from the Pokhara airstrip at 3,000 ft., the summit of Machhapuchhare is less than 20 miles away to the north, but without any intervening hills or major ridges, it soars fully 20,000 vertical feet above the Pokhara plain. And in the bottom of the Kali Gandaki gorge, the Jomsom trail winds through the deepest river canyon in the world where the variations are even more dramatic.

This booklet is primarily a collection of detailed descriptions of the major Pokhara-based trekking routes, giving special attention to the two most popular trails, to Jomsom and the Annapurna Sanctuary. High side treks leading up the spectacular walls of the Thak Khola canyon have also been described, including the routes to Muktinath, Tilichho Lake, Dhampus Pass, the north Annapurna base camp and the Dhaulagiri ice-fall. Finally, a description is given for the pleasant Ghorapani-Ghandrung trail which connects the Jomsom and the Annapurna Sanctuary treks.

These route descriptions are designed to provide unguided trekking groups with essential trail information and directions, including trekking times, elevations, suggested overnight stops and sources of local food and accommodations. Introductory sections on trekking permits, equipment, altitude sickness and travel connections to Pokhara have been included to aid in the preparation for a trek, and each major route description is preceeded by a general description of the area containing specific information about the weather, timing and any special preparation which may be required.

The descriptions are based largely on first-hand experience on the trail of this region, but they also contain information from a variety of sources. They have benefited from generous help of Mr. Dawa Norbu of the Mountain Travels, Kathmandu, who has made available much information collected by the agency over the years as well as his own considerable knowledge and expertise.

Trekking Permits and Visa Extensions

Before travelling to areas other than the Kathmandu Valley, Pokhara and Tiger Tops Lodge in the Chitawan District, special permission from the Central Immigration Office must be obtained in addition to a visa extension valid for the duration of the trip. This permission takes the form of a trekking permit which identifies the trekker by name, photograph and passport number and lists the specific itinerary for which the permit is valid. The trekking permit is examined in the field at police checkposts, encountered every few days along the Jomsom trail, where a record is made of the trekker's arrival and where notes may be entered on the permit itself.

Trekking permits and visa extensions are issued only by the Central Immigration Office, Ram Shah Path, Kathmandu. When completing the application forms, it is important to be as specific as possible in listing the proposed itinerary; for the widest possible latitude, list the most remote points on all the Pokhara-based trekking routes, and request a visa extension long enough to provide a comfortable margin for trekking at a leisurely pace. The forms must be accompanied by two passport-size photographs, and an application fee of 1 rupee is assessed.

After submitting the completed application forms, allow 24 hours for processing. Central Immigration is closed on Saturday and all other government holidays.

Visas
You may get visa extensions totalling a maximum of only three months for each entry into Nepal.

Trekking Equipment

Although equipment requirements are minimal for the simple round trip to Jomsom where comfortable local accommodation is found all along the way, all the higher Pokhara-based routes lead into uninhabited country where insufficiently equipped trekkers may be unable to proceed safely. The proper choice of equipment is important; it can mean the difference between an exciting and satisfying trek and a cold, painful and ultimately unsuccessful one. And the choice can be difficult to make, since whatever comfort may be derived from each item must be weighed against the physical cost of carrying it.

Certain basic trekking equipment is essential on all routes described in this booklet; the general suggestions which follow are aimed at this minimum requirement. Special food and equipment needs for treks to high Thak Khola passes and to the Annapurna Sanctuary are mentioned here also; they are discussed further in the introduction to the individual route descriptions.

Footwear

Shoes and socks are a trekkers most important pieces of equipment. Ill-fitting shoes can rapidly turn every step into torture, and with the additional weight of a 10- or 20-kilo load pressing down at each step, they may cause serious injury to the feet. In general, shoes should be well-worn and comfortable, providing solid support to the feet and ankles. Some trekkers walk in low-cut sneakers or other light shoes, and while they may be sufficient on much of the approach route to Jomsom, sturdier shoes are definitely required for treks to the Annapurna Sanctuary and the high Thak Khola passes where moraines and ice will be encountered. The best shoes for general use are middle-weight hiking shoes, at least ankle high, with Vibram soles, but a lighter pair should also be carried for use around camp, at low altitudes and as a back-up should the heavier pair prove uncomfortable.

If attempting to reach altitudes above 13,000 ft., in winter when camps must be made in the snow, even heavier shoes are desirable. In these circumstances, shoes should have an insulating inner sole to protect the feet from the often sudden and damaging effects of frostbite.

Socks serve the double purpose of cushioning the feet and preventing the accumulation of moisture on the skin which rapidly leads to blisters. At least two pairs of heavy socks should be worn, with a third light cotton pair next to the skin. A liberal dusting of shoes, socks and feet with foot-powder, changing to dry socks every day, will prevent most blisters. Carry at least one complete change of socks, and take more if travelling in wet weather.

Backpack

The standard H-frame pack is the best design for general trekking use, although some prefer the A-frame style, often of European manufacture. A large selection of packsacks is available for sale or rent in Kathmandu, including Kelty packs, one of the best of the H-frame styles.

Consider the weight of the empty packsack itself — some are unnecessarily heavy — and choose one with a bag large enough to accommodate the entire load; any equipment tied on the outside of the frame may be damaged in falls or when stored on top of the bus during the ride to Pokhara.

Bedding

A heavyweight down sleeping bag, preferably a mummy-bag which covers the head is necessary when sleeping above 10,000 ft. in this region. For the Jomsom trek, however, a lighter 3- to 4-lb. down bag is sufficient; the Thak Khola hotels will provide blankets on request. In early fall and late spring, the lighter sleeping bag may also be warm enough for middle-altitude treks up to 13,000 ft. if a good down coat is available to sleep in when necessary. An insulating foam ground pad is essential above 10,000 ft. to prevent excessive heat loss to the ground at night. Always carry a waterproof groundsheet, a plain plastic sheet is enough, to keep bedding clean and dry.

Rain Gear

Those attempting to reach high altitudes in this region may make the approach trek at the tail end of the monsoon in the last weeks of September or the return trek during the first weeks of the monsoon season in late spring; in either case, wet weather can be expected. In addition to the waterproof anorak, extra plastic sheets should be carried to cover packsacks when walking and to serve as groundsheets. Waterproof boot dressing and extra change of pants and socks should also be carried during these periods.

Clothing

No matter what the season, a wide range of temperatures is likely to be encountered in the course of a normal trekking day, and clothing should be chosen with an eye to its versatility as well as its warmth. A lightweight shirt and walking shorts should be included in the clothing kit; all routes described in this booklet include some low-altitude stretches which may be hot even in winter.

For use in a wide range of middle and high altitudes, include a pair of bluejeans or woollen pants, a heavy high-necked sweater and an anorak, preferably waterproof to double as a raincoat. The combination of anorak or wind jacket worn over a heavy sweater is unusually versatile; it is warm enough for all daytime use when walking in above- freezing weather.

When the sun goes down at altitudes above 10,000 ft., temperatures drop precipitously; sub-freezing temperatures must be expected at night on the Thak Khola side trips and in the Annapurna Sanctuary. For any trek above the 10,000-ft. level — anything other than a simple round trip to Jomsom — carry a down jacket, a set of long underwear, an extra pair of long pants, a heavy shirt and a pair of gloves or mittens. A wool knit cap should be carried on all treks to protect the head from both the cold and the high altitude sun.

When trekking above 13,000 ft. during the coldest winter months of December, January and early February, conditions cold enough to require even heavier clothing will be encountered. In this situation, an expedition-quality down coat with a hood and a wind jacket and wind pants may provide considerable comfort in the evenings and early mornings. Down pants are probably unnecessary except at very high altitudes in the dead of winter.

Map and Compass

A map and compass are absolutely essential on trips through uninhabited country or in high, rugged terrain. But even in low country on an easily followed trail, they will add greatly to the enjoyment of a trek by combating the "corridor effect", the tendency to confine one's attention to the route immediately ahead, unmindful of the surrounding country.

The Mandala trekking map entitled "Pokhara to Jomsom", locally drawn and blueprinted by International Graphic Arts, Kathmandu, is still the best map available for day-to-day trail use. On a scale of 1 inch to 2 miles, it covers the entire area described in this booklet and is designed especially for the needs of trekkers, it is available in Kathmandu in most book-stores and trekking houses.

The only other map which covers this area which is available to the public is the west half of a two-sheet map of Nepal based

11

on information collected from 1924 to 1927 by the survey of India. Entitled "Nepal 1:506,880, West Sheet," it is published by D Survey, Ministry of Defence, U.K. (1967). It covers all of west Nepal, but because it lacks detail, it is not very useful as a trail guide. It is particularly untrustworthy in its depiction of the area around Dhampus Pass and Hidden Valley.

Medical Kit

Apart from the well-equipped Shining Hospital in Pokhara, operated by a staff of foreign missionaries, a government hospital in Jomsom and a Rescue Aid at Manang there are no medical facilities of importance to trekkers on the routes described in this booklet; therefore, a medical kit containing first aid supplies and medicines for the treatment of colds, infection and intestinal complaints is an essential piece of trekking equipment. The following items should definitely be included.

Boroline Cream	This is another preparation for the prevention of sunburn.
Multifungin Powder	A foot powder for the prevention of blisters and fungus infection.
Aspirin or APC	Thirty to 50 tablets for headache, muscle pain and fever.
Tetracycline Hydrochloride	Thirty 250-mg. capsules. A broad spectrum antibiotic mainly for the control of severe respiratory infection.
Lomotil and Streptomagma	For the treatment of diarrhoea and dysentry.
Tincture of Iodine (2% solution)	Eight to 12 drops per litre for the purification of drinking water.
Sterile gauze and adhesive tape Band-aids	At least one roll each, shared between two trekkers. Ten to 20 small adhesive bandages for use on blisters and small wounds.
Elastic bandage	In case of muscle or tendon strain.
Antibiotic ointment	Bacitracin or Polymixin B for minor skin infections.

Ophthalmic ointment	For treatment of conjunctivitis.
Dristan tablets or Pheny-phrine hydrochloride nasal spray.	Decongestants for stuffy nose or inflamed sinuses.
Codeine	Ten to 20 15-mg. tablets for relief of pain and as a cough suppressant.

The contents of this medical kit will be in demand among villagers along the trails, many of whom can be helped by trekkers with some health or medical experience. But medical treatment of local people, especially those with severe systemic illnesses, should be undertaken with caution. Beyond treatment of cuts and minor infections and the dispensing of aspirin, there may be little one can do other than to assist the person in reaching a medical facility.

Other essential Trekking Items

Needle and thread	Soap
Spoon	Toilet paper
Sharp knife	Sun hat/cap

Candles and matches (to start a fire in an emergency).
Water bottle (at least 1 litre capacity).
Sunglasses (essential above 12,000 ft. or in snow).

Optional Equipment

Trekkers may wish to carry a number of other items which, while useful on certain treks, do not really qualify as minimum essential trekking equipment. Many people, particularly those on elaborate pre-arranged treks, choose to carry an entire camp over the route to Jomsom, including food, cooking utensils, stove, fuel and tent. While this kind of equipment is not necessary in order to reach Jomsom or the Annapurna Sanctuary during the normal trekking season, it has a number of advantages. Eliminating the dependence on local supplies of food and shelter, trekkers are able to stay for extended periods above the last occupied settlements, establishing their camps at points dictated more by preference and acclimatization level than the locations of population centers.

This level of preparation also opens up areas that would otherwise remain inaccessible. Notably Dhampus Pass, Tilichho Lake, the north Annapurna base camp and, to some extent, the Sanctuary. The cost of the equipment and supplies and the difficulties of managing and equipping porters are the primary disadvantages of this style of travel. Tents, stoves and cooking utensils are available in Kathmandu from shops which often offer equipment for rent as well as for sale. Kerosene for Primus stoves should be bought in Kathmandu and tested before beginning the trek; outside Kathmandu, kerosene is often so full of impurities it cannot be used.

Food and equipment requirements are discussed further in the introduction to the individual route descriptions. Other items for consideration: Flashlight, flea powder, insect repellent, writing materials, towel and leather-sewing awl with strong nylon thread.

Altitude Sickness

Trekkers who undertake a rapid ascent above 10,000 ft. may experience some of the symptoms of altitude sickness, also known as acute mountain sickness (AMS)- or, in its most severe forms, acute pulmonary or cerebral edema. This condition can be extremely serious, even fatal, for those who fail to heed the warning signals and continue to ascend in the presence of severe symptoms. Because the Jomsom trail is too low to provide a chance for acclimatization on the outward route, those who plan one of the high Thak Khola side trips should be especially wary of the danger.

The underlying physiological causes of altitude sickness are complex and not fully understood, but the development of symptoms parallels the body's attempt to adapt to the considerably reduced concentration of oxygen at high altitudes. The mild symptoms experienced first — shortness of breath, tiredness, headache and increased urine output — affect nearly everyone as they begin the process of acclimatization. Continued rapid ascent beyond the body's ability to adjust, however, may induce a total breakdown in the acclimatization process, resulting in more severe symptoms: an abrupt decrease in urine output, gross fatigue, severe headache, severe cough, wet bubbly breathing, a sense of fullness in the lungs, or delirium and confusion.

The breakdown in the body's adaptive mechanism is usually signalled by a marked reduction in urine output. Should this or any of the more serious symptoms occur, the most important life-saving treatment is to descend immediately to the last point before onset of severe symptoms. If the symptoms disappear after 48 hours, then the ascent can be continued at a slow pace. In cases of severe pulmonary edema, administration of oxygen, if available, and Lasix (one to three 40 mg. tablets per day) during the descent may provide relief. Lasix is a strong diuretic, and it should be employed only in a serious medical emergency, and only when an adequate supply of drinking water is available to replace lost fluids.

The more severe symptoms of altitude sickness can be prevented in almost all cases by regulating the speed of ascent to a rate of not more than 1,000 ft., per day above 10,000 ft., but this is almost impossible for the majority of trekkers who do not carry food, fuel and shelter with them and have to reach certain overnight objectives at the end of each day. At the very least, schedule one rest day for acclimatization at every 3,000 ft. level and maintain a daily intake of 3 to 4 quarts of fluids.

It is important to remember that mild symptoms are commonly experienced by all high-altitude trekkers, and they are not cause for alarm. But severe symptoms cannot be ignored: descend at once, as rapidly as possible, to an altitude where the acclimatization process can resume.

Kathmandu to Pokhara

By Bus

At least eight buses leave from Kathmandu for Pokhara every morning between 6.30 and 9.30 a.m. Three of the buses leave from the busyard on the north side of Kathmandu City Hall which is directly across the Tundikhel, the grassy parade ground, from the RNAC building on Kanti Path; one bus leaves from the company's ticket office under the tower beside the Kathmandu General Post Office.

Probably the fastest and most comfortable bus, however, is the express mail bus which leaves every morning from inside the post office compound; the ticket agent can be found on the sidewalk beside the post office. The ride takes 7 or 8 hours, and tickets presently cost around Rs.35/- one way. Although seats are sold right up to the hour of departure, book tickets a day in advance to get good seats. The lunch stop is at Mugling. Well known for its Nepalese food.

By Plane

Royal Nepal Airlines Corporation operates regularly scheduled flights to Pokhara seven days a week. Departure is at 9.10 a.m., and a one-way ticket costs Rs.460/- plus Rs.10 Airport Tax. The flight offers a close up view of Ganesh, Manaslu and Annapurna ranges, there is no discount for round-trip fares. Book tickets well in advance at the RNAC booking office at the intersection of New Road and Kanti Path.

Accommodation

In Pokhara, a variety of accommodation can be found in three general areas: a group of expensive Western-style hotels and a few cheaper Tibetan hotels are located near the airport; in the busy Pokhara bazaar 2 miles north of the airport, good accommodation is available at modest prices at the Yak Hotel next to the Pokhara Post Office; and the least expensive rooms are found in the series of bungalows and lodges on the banks of the Phewa Tal.

Pokhara via Lete and Marpha to Jomsom

The route from Pokhara to Jomsom up the Kali Gandaki River passes through a gap in the Himalayan barrier in the bottom of the deepest river canyon in the world. Penetrating between the Annapurna and Dhaulagiri ranges at a point where the principal peaks are only 20 miles apart, the trail leaves the lush south-slope rhododendron forests, winds through a breathtaking gorge nearly four miles deep and merges in the semi-arid Thak Khola canyon, an Inner Himalayan valley which gradually rises northward to merge with the Tibetan plateau beyond the desolate windblown hills of Mustang.

The walls of the upper canyon are tremendous snow-covered ridges sweeping northward from Annapurna and Dhaulagiri, bracketing the valley with ice cliffs and glaciers. The trail passes close under the nearly vertical slopes of Dhaulagiri and the Dhaulagiri icefall — there is no other place in the country where such a stunning display of high mountain scenery can be seen from such low altitudes.

The people of the Thak Khola are almost exclusively of Tibetan cultural heritage, including the Thakalis, a group of adaptive and shrewd traders whose ancient migration patterns have carried them southward all the way to the **terai**. The Thak Khola trail is still an important trade route; colourful heavily laden donkey caravans driven by Tibetan traders are a common sight. The trail is wide and easy to follow, and it is not as physically demanding as many other trekking routes; the highest point on the way is 9,500 ft. at Ghorapani pass, and above Tatopani, the trail ascends gradually along the Kali Gandaki to an altitude of 8,900 ft. at Jomsom.

Equipment

Unless one of the higher Thak Khola side trips is to be attempted, the Jomsom trip requires no special supplies or preparation beyond the basic trekking equipment already mentioned. Because of its popularity as a trekking route, many comfortable local inns and tea shops are found along the way. They provide pleasant accommodation and good morning and evening meals, and they often sell tinned and manufactured goods up from Pokhara.

Timing

A simple Pokhara to Jomsom round trip is low enough to be undertaken without difficulty any time between October and May. The period from October through December provides the clearest skies and the best mountain views. During December, January and early February, however, cold weather makes some of the higher side trips difficult or impossible; deep snow and ice will be found above 13,000 ft. The weather warms up considerably in late February, and in March, April and May, the rhododendron forests bloom around Ghorapani ridge.

October, November and March are the best months for the trip; later in the spring and summer, clouds form in the mountain early in the day, obscuring distant views. The round trip to Jomsom can be made in two weeks, but for those who wish to make stop-overs in interesting villages and to do a thorough job of exploring the country, it may take more, nearly 20 days.

Pokhara (2,912′) to Naudanda (4,800′): 5 hours.*

From the Pokhara airport, take a bus or taxi to the upper end of the bazaar; the turnaround near the Shining Hospital and the National Multipurpose High School marks the real start of the Jomsom trek.

Follow the wide jeep track past the high school and beyond as it descends into the shallow canyon of the Seti Khola and follow the river under low cliffs along the west bank. About 20 minutes beyond the turnround, cross the Yangdi Khola which comes in on the left; during dry-weather months, both rivers will be low and clear. One hour beyond the end of the bazaar, the road climbs out of the river bottom to the **Tibetan Camp,** the first structure in **Lower Hyengja** (3,500′). Here, Tibetan refugees operate a co-operative handicraft center in which Tibetan carpets, boots and other garments are made for sale. Visitors may observe carding, spinning and dyeing of wool and the weaving and cutting of carpets.

---

*The subdivision in the body of the route descriptions which follow are intended primarily for readability and are not necessarily recommendations for a daily itinerary. Each one, however, ends at a convenient overnight stop, and each section can be covered on one day. Times are meant to reflect actual walking time with an allowance for short rests but not for lunch stops or longer breaks.

The road leaves the Seti Khola beyond the Tibetan camp of Hyengja on the ridge separating the Seti Khola from the Yangdi Khola. It is a green and peaceful place, especially along the wide grassy trail joining the lower village and **Upper Hyengja** (3,600'). Several pleasant tea shops are located in this section.

Beyond here, the road descends into the shallow Yangdi Khola valley which is lined with terraces for rice cultivation. A temporary trail, used during the fall and winter when the rice terraces are dry, stays near the river as the valley widens out; in wet weather, follow the permanent trail along the irrigation ditch around the north side of the valley. The few houses of **Suikhet** (3,600') are reached 1 hour beyond the last houses of Upper Hyengja. The first house on the right is a hotel, and just beyond the village, a series of small bhattis, simple hillside inns often made of thatch or bamboo mats, offer cheap accommodation.

The trail continues near the river for half an hour beyond Suikhet, then it crosses to the south side of the valley where two tea shops are located at the start of a 1,200-ft. climb up the ridge dividing the Yangdi Khola valley from the short valley of the Harpan Khola. Phewa Tal and nearly the whole Harpan Khola valley are visible from the south side of the ridge, and to the north, Machhapuchhare and the Annapurna Himal are spread out grandly on the skyline. **Naudanda** lies along the top of this ridge about 2 hours beyond Suikhet; the village contains a number of hotels with English signboards, including the comfortable Mahendra Lodge.

A pause for tea at Sarangkot, north west of Pokhara
(Photo P. Morris)

Naudanda (4,800') to Birethanti (3,500'): 5½ hours

At the far end of the Naudanda Bazaar, the trail splits; a wide low trail angles to the left, and an obscure track climbs a small hill to the right. Both branches join again shortly, but the right-hand trail is somewhat shorter and less stony. Continue westward 1½ hours to the first houses of **Khare** (5,600'), the largest village on Kaski Danda. Here, the trail shifts over to the north side of the ridge at the head of the Yangdi Khola watershed, and just beyond the village it crosses a small creek to begin its descent into the Modi Khola valley. A British agricultural research station and training center is located about 20 minutes beyond Khare. Here, Nepalese returning from service in the British Ghurka Regiments are given training in agriculture under the Gurkha Repatriation Program.

Less than an hour beyond the centre of Khare, the trail passes through the village of **Lumle** (5,100') and in another hour it reaches **Chandrakot** (5,124'), a small village with hotels, shops and a school perched on the end of the ridge 1,600 ft. above the Modi Khola. The viewpoint at the west end of the village offers a fine panorama in all directions. To the north, the Modi Khola emerges through a narrow gorge from the Annapurna Sanctuary; south of Birethanti, the canyon widens out into a maze of ridges and tributary valleys with dozens of small villages perched on the canyon walls in unlikely places. Across the canyon to the west, the Bhurungdi Khola flows down from near Ghorapani Pass, the village of Ulleri can be seen in the distance where the trail leaves the Bhurungdi Khola and starts the climb to Ghorapani. Sunrise and sunset views from here are particularly fine.

Descend steeply westward from Chandrakot into the Modi Khola canyon. This stretch, although short, should be taken slowly to avoid injury to the knees. Nearing the river, turn downstream to a bridge, and cross into **Birenthanti**, 1½ hours from Chandrakot. Birenthanti contains a number of shops and hotels as well as a police checkpost. Many trekkers choose to spend an extra day in this pleasant village exploring the bazaar and the two beautiful rivers which meet here. Twenty minutes upstream on the Bhurungdi Khola, a large waterfall plunges into a clear pool under bamboo-covered cliffs; just upstream, a series of small waterfalls is worth exploring.

The village of Khare (5,600 ft.) lies along the narrow crest of the Kaski Danda ridge.

Along the lower Bhurungdi Khola at elevation below 4,000 ft., there are many spots ideal for bathing, washing clothes or just relaxing in the sun. This waterfall is only a few minutes above Birethanti.

23

Birethanti (3,500 ft.), at the confluence of the Mhodi Khola and the Bhurungdi Khola, as a quiet and restful place where trekkers are often tempted to stay over a day or two.

Birethanti (3,500') to Ghorapani (9,300'): 9 hours

The main trail goes through the Birethanti bazaar and follows the Bhurungdi Khola upstream along the north-east bank. After 40 minutes, it comes out above the last falls to a group of **bhattis** serving the donkey caravans. Above here, it crosses to the west bank briefly to avoid a cliff then recrosses and continues up the east bank. Two hours from Birethanti, a small cluster of houses called **Sudhami** is reached; the village of **Hille** (4,800') lies about 45 minutes beyond it. **Tirkhedhunga** (4,900'), a small village with good tea shops, is just a few minutes beyond Hille.

The trail descends and crosses the river beyond Tirkhedhunga, then it begins a steep 2,000-ft. climb up a series of stone steps; it takes 1½ to 2 hours to reach the trailside tea shops and hotels at **Ulleri** (6,800'). Above here, the trail is less steep, but it continues to climb in a steady uphill grade with a few steep stretches. It soon enters the dense forests which cover the Ghorapani ridge for miles in all directions; rhododendrons and related species such as Daphe and azalea dominate at the lower elevations, giving away to stands of giant conifers above 10,000 ft.

Climbing generally north through the forest, cross three small creeks on the bridges, climbing up out of the ravines each time. Three hours beyond Ulleri, the little settlement of **Thante** (8,000') is located in a clearing in the forest. Overnight accommodation can be found in at least two of the half-dozen huts here, and a good campsite is located on the hill behind the first group of huts.

Continue to climb through the thick rhododendron forest to **Ghorapani**, 1½ hours beyond Thante. The village, consisting of only about a dozen buildings, lies in a clearing 200 ft. below Ghorapani Pass (9,500'), 15 minutes further up the trail. The pass lies in a saddle on the great forested ridge projecting southward from Annapurna South (23,683'), about 10 miles away to the northeast. There are at least two good hotels here, and an elaborate new one is under construction.

An interesting and scenic route, described in pp. 68-69 connects Ghorapani with Ghandrung in the Modi Khola canyon to the east, making possible a combination of the Jomsom and Annapurna Sanctuary treks without returning to Birethanti.

The best views of Annapurna (left, in pictures above and below) and Annapurna South can be seen from Pun Hill near Ghorapani Pass. In the light of the rising sun, it is one of the finest mountain views in the region.

Pun Hill (10,500')

Because Ghorapani and Ghorapani Pass both lie close under forested hills to the north, the Himalayas are not visible from either place. However, one of the best viewpoints in the region, Pun Hill, is located on the ridgetop southwest of the pass about 45 minutes' climb above the village. When the sky is clear, usually early in the morning, the view of Annapurna South is unobstructed, and it can be studied from top to bottom from very close. Annapurna, the Nilgiris, Dhaulagiri, Tukche, Himchuli and a bit of the top of Machhapuchhare also appear powerfully outlined against the sky.

To reach Pun Hill, take the well-marked path which splits off the main trail near the upper end of the village, cross the grassy field on the left and climb up through the forest onto steep open hillsides. The trail switches back and forth up the steep lower section, reaching many false summits, and at the top, passes through a conifer forest before coming out onto a round grassy knoll often used as a camping spot. There is now a good and much used lodge half way up to Pun Hill top. Many people make this climb before dawn to watch the rising sun light the peaks in pinks and oranges — truly a magnificent sight.

Improvements

Contrary to belief in some quarters, publishers of guide books invariably welcome information and suggestions likely to improve subsequent editions.

We cordially invite users of this book to make notes on the trail and to write to us giving the relevant page number or numbers and suggestions as to what might be done to effect improvements.

It is a long standing tradition in mountaineering and trekking circles that one does what one can to help those who follow and readers may care to join us in helping to develop this title.

We in turn will be pleased to send complimentary copies of the next edition to senders of the most useful letters.

Ghorapani (9,300') to Tatopani (4,000'): 6½ hours.

Follow the main trail up to the pass, and start the long descent into Kali Gandaki canyon from a small group of buildings at the stone cairns on the summit. Although the trail is not steep beyond the pass, the north-facing slopes are often covered with snow and ice, particularly early or late in the year, and it can be slow going for the first 1,000 ft. About an hour below the top, the village of **Chitre** (7,700') is spread out in clusters along the trail; pass through **Phalate** (7,500') a few minutes beyond the last houses of Chitre.

The centre of **Sikha** (6,600') is reached in 3 hours from Ghorapani Pass; it contains several shops, a post office, a school and some government buildings including a small health post. Beyond Sikha, the descent becomes steeper and the trail stonier. Pass the village of **Ghare** (5,800') in an hour, and descend steeply into the canyon, crossing the Ghar Khola on a high shaky wooden bridge.

In the bottom of the Kali Gandaki canyon, the pine forests of the higher elevations are replaced by a low semi-arid vegetation under steep canyon walls and rocky cliffs. Beyond the Ghar Khola bridge the trail curves northward briefly and crosses the Kali Gandaki on a steel suspension bridge to the west bank; **Tatopani** lies on the narrow shelf beside the river a few minutes upstream from the bridge and about 2½ hours beyond Ghare.

Tatopani consists of several clusters of buildings separated by fields, and near the upper end of the village, several hotels offer good accommodation and excellent food; well stocked shops are found throughout the village. Tatopani which means "hot water" in Nepali, is famous for its hot springs which are found on both sides of the river near the water's edge. They are sulphur rings heated by geothermic processes — just right for a hot bath. Local people use the water for therapeutic bathing and as a tonic, drinking directly from the springs. One of the best bathing spots is across the river. It is reached by crossing the river on a bamboo bridge north of the town then walking down-stream a few hundred yards along the riverbank. There is a well built pool with possibilities to wash clothes, right behind the Travellers Lodge. Other springs are located on the west bank near the mouth of the creek below the Kamala Lodge.

Loaded yaks pass under the Rupse Chhahara waterfall on their way north up the canyon.

29

Traders from Mustang District are constantly on the move up and down the Jomsom Trail. This girl and her brother are selling herbs from Pokhara as they make their way northward after a trip to the lowlands.

In the narrowest part of the Kali Gandaki gorge, the stretch between Titre and Ghasa, the spectacular west bank trail is chiselled into the face of the vertical cliffs high above the river.

31

Tatopani (4,000′) to Ghasa (6,600′): 6¾ hours

The trail continues upstream beneath the sheer cliffs of the canyon wall. About 30 minutes above Tatopani, pass the intersection of the Kali Gandaki and the Miritsi Khola, cascading down through a steep-walled gorge from glaciers between Annapurna and Tilichho Peak to the North-east. Annapurna was climbed by the French in 1950, the first successful ascent of an 8,000-meter peak, from a camp on the headwaters of this stream. The trail passes this point high on the canyon wall as it goes through a small hand made tunnel to avoid a sheer cliff. The village of **Dana** (4,800′) is reached 2-3 hours beyond Tatopani. A police checkpost and several government offices are located here as well as a tea shop and hotel in the upper village.

Continue up and down along the hillside for about 45 minutes to the small village of **Titre** (5,000′). Just north of the main part of the village, pass a comfortable Tibetan tea shop; 5 minutes beyond this shop, the trail reaches a major junction under the **Rupse Chhahara waterfall.** This spectacular waterfall is formed as a tributary creek plunges down from high up on the cliffs to power a series of small grain mills near the trail. Cross the creek on the wooden bridge, and immediately arrive at the fork in the trail.

One branch climbs abruptly to the left and continues north along the west canyon wall, while the other descends to a bridge across the Kali Gandaki and goes up the east side of the river. The two trails each offering a unique trekking experience, join again below Ghasa, about 3 hours to the north. The west bank trail is the older and more primitive trail; it is carved out of the rock on vertical cliffs high above the river. In places it is like a tunnel in the rock with the right-hand side removed; several rickety bridges span gaps between ledges. During rainy weather there is some danger from falling rocks and slides in this section. The east bank route, in contrast, is a newer trail made possible by the recent construction of a permanent bridge below Ghasa, and it is wider, higher and safer for pack animals.

West Bank Trail from Titre to Ghasa: 3 hours
Turn left up the ravine beside the waterfall just after crossing the bridge, and climb steeply up the hillside a few hundred feet before turning back upriver. The trail remains high and passes the village of **Kabre** (5,900') after 30 minutes; it is just below the steepest part of the gorge. Beyond here, the trail is chiseled into the face of the vertical cliffs high above the river. This stretch should be taken slowly and carefully; although the bridges are solid and the footing secure, gale-force winds perpetually howl through this narrow gorge, and the noise and constant buffeting can make it difficult to concentrate on the trail. After about 2 hours in the gorge, the canyon begins to widen a little, and the trail descends into a gravel bar beside the river where a wooden bridge joins the east bank and west bank trails. **Ghasa** is 30 minutes upstream from here.

East Bank Trail from Titre to Ghasa: 2½ hours
Continue along the wide main trail past the tea shops at the creek, and gradually descend to the bridge over the turbulent Kali Gandaki. On the east bank, the trail stays fairly low at first, passing through a small village 20 minutes beyond the bridge. After this, the trail starts to climb; eventually, it goes steeply up in switchbacks through a lush forest where colonies of large grey and white monkeys are often seen on the trees. Staying high, the trail then traverses the steepest section of the gorge and descends to the gravel bar and the small bridge leading back to the west bank about 2 hours beyond Titre bridge. This small bridge is a temporary structure used only when the river is low, but a few minutes further up the trail, a newly completed steel suspension bridge provides a more secure crossing.

Ghasa, which contains tea shops and hotels, is the first Thakali village on the trek, and it marks the end of the subtropical vegetation and the beginning of the conifer forests which characterize the canyon above here. The wind is noticably stronger and colder now, and the canyon begins to widen out approaching the deepest section near Lete.

The first close-up view of Dhaulagiri is a good one; it comes a few minutes above the village of Ghasa.

34

Ghasa (6,600') to Lete (8,000'): 2¾ hours

From Ghasa, the trail climbs steadily but not steeply, and it soon enters pine forests, then mixed conifer stand later on. After about an hour, the canyon widens further, and the trail rounds a bend to expose a magnificent close-up view of Dhaulagiri and the Dhaulagiri icefall. Across the river, a huge cliff carved out of loose sediments rises a thousand feet above the river. When the wind is blowing hard, it raises plumes of dust high in the air from the cliff and dislodges boulders which go crashing down into the canyon. The Dhaulagiri ice-fall often adds to the powerful noise as it rumbles and shifts.

Nearing Lete, the trail descends into the small tributary ravine of the Lete Khola which enters the Kali Gandaki half a mile away on the right. Cross the stream on a wooden bridge, and climb up the far bank in loose boulders and sediments to gain the top of a flat river terrace. Follow the wide trail to the left over a small

hill, and reach the first buildings of **Lete** on the edge of the Lete Khola ravine. The first building is a hotel, and it can be reached comfortably in 2½ hours from Ghasa.

Lete is strung out almost 2 miles along this river terrace. It is divided into two sections; the upper one (8,400') is also known as Kalopani. Across the Kali Gandaki from lower Lete, the interesting village of **Chhoya** is located on the delta of the Pangbu Khola. South-east of Chhoya, a series of trails leads into a thick jungle along the top of the cliffs which are visible approaching Lete from the south. Colonies of large monkeys as well as other wildlife live along these cliffs.

A Thakali woman weaving a rug in the sun at Ghasa.
(Photo P. Morris)

35

Lete (8,000') to Tukche (8,500'): 4 hours
Climb gradually through the village of Lete along the gently sloping river terrace for nearly an hour before reaching **Kalopani** (8,400'), a small settlement on the bank of the river. Kalopani lies at the foot of an enormous gravel bar, stretching, with numerous interruptions, well beyond Jomsom. There is a bridge here over the Thak Khola, as the river is now called, and either the east or west bank may be followed to Tukche. The east bank trail is more direct, but when the river is high in the spring, the crossing back to the west bank cannot easily be made. The west bank trail is slightly longer but easier to follow, and it passes through the interesting villages of Larjung and Khopang on the way. It is worthwhile to vary the route, going up one bank and returning on the other.

East Bank Trail from Kalopani to Tukche: 3 hours
Cross the Kalopani bridge to the east bank, and head upstream on a trail that stays above the gravel bar. Pass the village of **Dhumpu** spread out on a rocky hillside 15 minutes beyond the bridge, and pass another settlement below the trail 30 minutes further on where the trail leaves the river briefly to climb over the shoulder of a forested ridge. Climbing over this shoulder, the trail avoids a narrow place on the gravel bar where the river cuts under steep cliffs. About 20 minutes after starting the climb, the trail descends again and forks where it meets the gravel.

One trail stays on the bank and skirts the gravel bar, while the other strikes out onto the gravel and proceeds upstream along the east side. In dry weather, the route across the bar is more direct. After little more than half an hour from this fork, a bridge is reached which crosses the river to the village of **Larjung** (8,400') on the west bank. When the river is low, however, remain on the east side of the gravel bar all the way to Tukche before crossing.

Along the east side of the gravel bar, the views of Annapurna, Dhaulagiri and Tukche peak are tremendous. The wind can be very strong out on the bar, and in the afternoons it raises great clouds of dust and can actually move small pebbles along the ground. About 1 hour beyond the Larjung bridge and 3 hours beyond Lete, the trail crosses back to the west bank at **Tukche** on a series of low log bridges to the east side of the bar all the way to Tukche to avoid being trapped by shallow streams below the log bridges.

The Nilgiri Peaks tower over the Tukche village gate; directly behind them lies the north Annapurna Glacier basin.

Near Larjung, the trail passes close under the east side of Dhaulagiri.

West Bank Trail from Kalopani to Tukche: 3 hours
Continue upstream from Kalopani on the main trail along the west edge of the gravel bar. In dry weather, the most direct route turns out onto the gravel bar below cliffs at its narrowest part; keeping to the west side, it is possible to get through this section with dry feet if the river is low. The trail then crosses the rubble-strewn delta of a small creek just below the village of **Sokung** (8,500') which is reached in less than an hour from Kalopani. Beyond Sokung, some stretches can be covered on the gravel bar, but the river makes it necessary to return to the main trail from time to time. After crossing one more tributary delta coming in from the left, the village of **Larjung** (8,400') is reached about half an hour beyond Sokung.

The fascinating Thakali villages of Larjung and Khopang are just a few minutes apart. The houses are built very close together and are completely enclosed with walls which often shelter a small open courtyard inside. Many buildings extend out over the trail and connect with buildings on the other side, forming tunnels through which the trail and village streets pass. The many architectural peculiarities of these villages seem to be aimed at achieving protection from the strong winds which constantly howl up the canyon across the gravel bar. On the cliffs beyond **Khopang,** rows of ancient caves contain Buddhist shrines and religious relics. Tukche is about 1½ hours' walk upstream from Larjung, and on the way, the trail passes a very old monastery called Rani Gomba, which is known for fine wall paintings of great age.

Tukche lies on a small alluvial fan formed by intersection of the Thak Khola and the Dhampus Khola which flows abruptly down from the east shoulder of Tukche Peak. A large Thakali town, it has been a trading centre on the route to Tibet since ancient times. Tukche contains three monasteries counting Rani Gomba Samba, the newer monastery on the north edge of town. A series of hotels and tea shops here cater to trekkers.

Gale force winds raise clouds of dust from the gravel bar at Tukche. Downstream, the steep southeast ridge of Dhaulagiri seems to block the lower Thak Khola canyon.

Tukche (8,500') to Jomsom (8,900'): 4 hours

Beyond Tukche, the trail stays up, on the west bank, and it is easy going except for the wind. The country appears arid and desolate now with junipers and small pines scattered on the mountainsides. Continue northward another hour, pass a bridge leading across the river to the monastery and the Tibetan handicraft center at **Chhairo.** Shortly afterward, the trail passes the Marpha Experimental farm, a government research center established in 1966 which specializes in the cultivation and introduction of fruits and vegetables not grown before in the area. From here, **Marpha** (8,760') is reached in half an hour.

Marpha is a large Thakali village containing an important monastery at its south end. The village is huddled on the leeward side of a ridge which gives it some protection from the wind, and a number of good hotels, notably the Mustang and Tilichho lodges, offer excellent accommodation.

North of Marpha, the trail is wide and easy to follow. Cross the delta of the Pongkyu Khola, and remain well away from the river beyond it. After about an hour, the trail passes a butte on the far side of the river; a bridge at its base provides an alternate return route from Jomsom down the east bank through Thini. Staying on the west bank, however, pass the mouth of the Longpoghyun Khola flowing down from Meso Kanto pass to the east. The village of Syang (8,900') is just a few minutes past the butte. The trail goes on to pass the Jomsom airstrip, reaching the first buildings of **Jomsom** an hour beyond Syang.

The main part of Jomsom is on the east bank of the river across a sturdy wooden bridge. Among the government offices here, there is a police station where the officials are conscientious in checking passports and trekking permits. The Nilgiri lodge next to the checkpost is a comfortable hotel. Jomsom also contains a small military post in radio communication with Kathmandu. A few hours of exploration immediately around Jomsom can be rewarding. A number of hot springs are found against the hillside west of the town, and picking through the stones on the bank of the river can be fascinating; it is not uncommon to find ammonite snail fossils.

Return from Jomsom via Thini to Marpha (9,500'): 3 hours

Returning southward toward Marpha, it is worthwhile to follow the east bank trail through Thini and past Dhumpa, crossing back to the west bank about 2 hours from Jomsom and less than an hour above Marpha. Follow the alleyways uphill to the east edge of Jomsom, and find the path to Thini at the base of the hill. Do not climb the little knoll at the base of the hill, but skirt the bottom around to the right. The path goes up on the hillside and remains fairly high, providing a good perspective of Jomsom and the valley around it.

About 45 minutes beyond Jomsom, enter the village of **Thini**, and circle left through the village into the rugged canyon of the Longpoghyun Khola. Work down to the bottom of the canyon through boulders and scree, and cross a small plateau in the center. The views upstream toward Meso Kanto are striking. The village of **Dhumpa** is high on the butte south of the creek. Circle under the base of the butte to the right to find the wooden bridge across the river to the west bank.

Lete to The North Annapurna Base Camp

The French expedition of 1950, finding the ascent of Dhaulagiri impossible, turned their attention to the north slopes of Annapurna. After a series of brilliant reconaissance efforts, they succeeded in moving their entire expedition to base camp on the north Annapurna glaciers at the head of the awesome Miritsi Khola gorges over an arduous route known as the 'Passage du 27 avril'. The base camp lies at the edge of a glacier basin ringed by Tilichho Peak and the Niligiri summits to the north and west and the great barrier of Annapurna on the south-east.

The basin is approached from Chhoya, a Thakali village on the east bank of the Thak Khola opposite Lete. The trail crosses the southern buttress of the Nilgiris at 14,000 ft., eventually reaching 16,000 ft. along the precipitous north wall of the upper Miritsi Khola canyon. The route is characterised by extremely steep slopes covered with loose rock, and it involves difficult passages along sheer cliffs above the Miritsi Khola gorge. In the gorge, the trail is sketchy and indistinct, sometimes disappearing entirely; a fresh snowfall can make the upper passages tricky and dangerous, and since the route descends into a basin with no low escape route, altitude sickness is an important hazard. The trek should be undertaken only by well-equipped and guided groups with at least some climbing experience.

Equipment and Timing

As for the high side treks to Meso Kanto and Dhampus pass, food, stove, fuel and shelter must be carried to reach the north Annapurna glacier basin. Food requirements will be large, amounting to between seven and 10 days per person, including guides and porters. Under conditions of fresh snow, the route can become very difficult in the upper portions; it should not be attempted later than November or earlier than April.

Lete (8,000') to Chhoya Deorali (8,000'): 3 hours

The trail to Chhoya, if approaching south of Lete, leaves the main Jomsom trail at the wooden bridge over the Lete Khola. Instead of climbing up to Lete, take the path to the right, up the Thak Khola, and cross the bridge over the river leading into the lower part of Chhoya. If approaching from north of Lete, cross the Thak Khola to the east bank at the Kalopani bridge, and follow the trail southward for about 1 hour to **Chhoya**. A number of local men from this village have had experience on the route; one should be engaged as a guide into the difficult country above here.

From Chhoya, the trail leads uphill onto the broad delta of the Pangbu Khola then turns south-east onto a pine forest littered with giant boulders and small clearings connected by a maze of pathways. The trail gradually climbs to the rounded shoulder of the low ridge dividing the Pangbu Khola and the Tangdung Khola then continues southeast to the top of the steep slopes which fall away into the canyon of the Tangdung Khola. The first night's camp should be made at the site of a shepherd's camp above the slopes north of the river.

Chhoya Deorali (8,000') to Shepherds' Camp (13,000) 8 hours

Make the steep descent into the canyon of the Tangdung Khola on a narrow track leading down along the cliffs into the river bottom. The stream is the last source of water for about a day and a half. After crossing it, ascend a practically vertical slab of rock in narrow switchbacks, and enter dense forests covering the very steep slopes above. Beyond the Tangdung Khola, the track ascends about 6,000 ft. in a lateral distance of only 2 miles. The trail continues through jungle, emerging into clearings now and then, generally heading eastward. Eventually the forest thins out, and the track begins a steep ascent up a long gully covered with loose stones. Camp above the top of this gully at about 13,000 ft. at a shepherds' camp, or, if time permits, ascend the last 1,000 ft. and camp at the pass.

Shepherds' Camp (13,000') to Hum Khola (14,000'): 4 or 5 hours:
From the shepherds' camp, turn northwest and climb toward a notch on the main ridge at 14,000 ft. This is the pass of 'April 27', marked by a **chorten.** From here, the trail continues to climb north east along the point of the ridge before going in under the crest and turning east to an altitude of about 15,000 ft. some 3 hours after the shepherds' camp. Now the trail descends into the canyon of the Hum Khola, a tributary of the Miritsi Khola and crosses it at about 14,000 ft.

Although the Miritsi Khola camp can be reached in one day from the shepherds' camp at 13,000 ft. if the weather is good and there is no snow on the trail, it would be a very long and exhausting day. A camp should be made at the Hum Khola for acclimatization purposes and to break up the long and difficult traverse along the gorge of the Miritsi Khola.

Hum Khola (14,000') to Miritsi Khola (13,000'): 6 hours
Beyond the Hum Khola, the trail climbs very steeply back out of the canyon and goes over a shoulder at 16,000 ft. on the rocky cliffside. The trail then traverses the rugged canyon wall, generally angling downward into the Miritsi Khola, but often climbing over the cliffs and obstructions. After crossing several small streams, the trail finally descends to the river at an elevation of about 13,000 ft.

Depending on the time of arrival at this point a camp may be made here beside the river. If time permits, however, cross the stream, and go up along the south bank to the terminal moraine of the north Annapurna glacier at about 13,700 ft. The 1950 base camp was located in a flat spot on the moraine north of the foot of the northwest spur of Annapurna.

From Marpha to Dhampus Pass and Hidden Valley

The western wall of the Thak Khola canyon is a tremendous snowcovered ridge surmounted by Dhaulagiri and Tukche Peak as well as numerous lesser peaks between 18,000 and 20,000 ft. in height. This barrier can be crossed during favourable weather conditions at a point west of Marpha known as Dhampus Pass (17,000'). Beyond this pass lies Hidden Valley, a high glacier basin running down to the north and bracketed by the ice ridges of the Dhaulagiri and Mukut Himals. This area was first explored by Maurice Herzog and the French expedition of 1950 in an unsuccessful attempt to locate a feasible route up Dhaulagiri.

The ascent of Dhampus Pass even under ideal conditions can be a difficult climb for even well-equipped and experienced trekkers. This pass is covered with a deep layer of snow most of the year, and because of the notoriously unpredictable weather near Dhaulagiri, camping in a Hidden Valley, where a sudden weather change might block the return to the Thak Khola canyon, cannot be recommended.

Timing and Equipment

The ascent can normally be made in early fall or in late spring during the two lulls between the winter storms and the summer monsoon; the best conditions are found in October and May. Even then snow and ice may be encountered above the upper Tukche yak pastures. The last shelter is located at about 13,000 ft., and to camp above here, food, tent, stove and fuel must be carried as well as substantial cold-weather clothing and bedding.

Altitiude sickness may be a limiting factor for those attempting to camp on Dhampus pass on the third day beyond Marpha. An intermediate camp between the upper Tukche yak pastures and the summit is recommended, and a descent should be started immediately should serious symptoms of altitude sickness develop.

46

Marpha (8,760') to Marpha Fields (12,000'): 4 hours

From Marpha, climb directly west up the steep eroded slopes behind the main part of the village. The trail climbs through a pine forest and emerges above the trees on a rocky promontory. Just beyond this point, reach **Marpha Fields,** an area cultivated by Villagers

from Marpha. There are several huts here where shelter can be found, and there are good camping spots with water nearby. Marpha fields can easily be reached in one day from Jomsom.

The main street of Marpha and its white-painted stone houses. An old woman carrying a wicker basket shuffles along as a brass urn slowly fills with water.
(Photo P. Morris)

Marpha Fields (12,000') to Tukche Yak Pastures (13,000'): 6 hours

From the upper part of the settlement at Marpha fields, follow the trail toward the south-west as it rounds the shoulder of two ridges; the first one is a spur, the second is the main ridge which forms the north wall of the Dhampus Khola canyon. In less than 2 hours from Marpha fields, turn the corner of the main ridge, and reach an area of open pastures (about 13,000') where the trail from Tukche comes up the point of the ridge to join the higher trail from Marpha.

Now the trail descends gradually as it turns into the canyon of the Dhampus Khola and heads north-west high on the canyon wall. The trail rises and falls along this steep and rocky cliffside, and in fresh snow conditions, the footing can be difficult. Beyond the last cliffs, as the valley begins to widen out, reach a good camping spot called **Tukche Yak Pastures.** There are four huts here which can be used for shelter, and water is available nearby.

Tukche (8,500') to Tukche Yak Pastures (13,000'): 8 or 9 hours
Tukche yak pastures can be reached in a single long day from Tukche rather than Marpha or Marpha fields. Although the Tukche trail is more direct when approaching the area from the south, it is steeper, rougher and more difficult to follow; the footing can be treacherous in places, particularly on the descent.

From the open field near the monastery at the north end of Tukche, a trail climbs straight north up the steep hillside in switchbacks. The climb becomes more gradual beyond the top of this first steep stretch as the trail continues north to the base of the high ridge which forms the north wall of the Dhampus Khola canyon. At the base of a high cliff beyond here, the trail swings to the right and climbs along the cliff, eventually emerging on top on the point of the main ridge. Follow the broad ridge north-west to its intersection with the main Marpha trail at 13,000 ft. Beyond this junction, 4 hours from Tukche, follow the main trail along the canyon wall to Tukche yak pastures, about 4 more hours to the west.

Tukche Yak Pastures (13,000') to Dhampus Pass (17,000'): at least 6 hours
Above this point, there is neither firewood nor shelter, and the trail is practically non-existent. To proceed to the pass, climb up the steep slopes north west of the pastures, and continue to head north-west, following the line of least resistance. The pass appears as a wide shallow depression flanked by a 19,800-ft. peak on the left. During late spring and early fall, there may be no snow in Hidden Valley north of the pass, but the descent beyond Dhampus pass should be undertaken only by well-equipped and experienced groups. In uncertain weather, camp on the pass, or ascend from Tukche Yak Pastures to the pass and return the same day.

Jomsom Via Kangbeni to Muktinath

One of the holiest and most famous pilgrimage destinations in Nepal is the temple of miraculous fire, Jwala Mai, in Muktinath (12,460'). Permission to visit Muktinath has traditionally been reserved for Hindu pilgrims; however, a recent selective granting of permits to Western tourists may indicate a loosening of this restriction. In order to pass the checkpost in Jomsom, it has, in the past, been necessary to have Muktinath specifically mentioned on the trekking permit. Check the current requirements in Kathmandu.

The route goes directly up the wide gravel bar north of Jomsom. Stay near the east side of the gravel, and climb up to the trail on the east bank when the river makes it necessary. About 2 hours beyond Jomsom, the trail crosses the Panda Khola and another small stream just beyond the Muktinath trail junction, comes into view. Reach the trail junction below the confluence of the Thak Khola and the Jhong Khola about 2½ jhours beyond Jomsom. Turn east up the south side of the Jhong Khola canyon, and start the climb of more than 3,000 ft. to Muktinath. It takes approximately 4½ hours, and the village of Khingar is passed about halfway. Between Khingar and Muktinath there are a number of small settlements along the trail.

Muktinath is protected from the fierce wind blowing in the Thak Khola canyon, and from here, the views of the canyon and the Dhaulagiri group amply justify the climb. In the temple of Jwala Mai, a small spring flows from the rock, and a burning jet of natural gas issues from the same opening. Thus, the miraculous fire burns on water, earth and stone, a demonstration of divine omnipotence. There is also a pagoda-style temple nearby containing an image of Vishnu. Beside the temple in a grove of trees, a sacred stream feeds 108 waterspouts carved in the shape of cows.

Jomsom to Meso Kanto Pass and Tilichho Lake

The walls of the Thak Khola canyon are formed by massive ridges extending northward from the Annapurna and Dhaulagiri ranges. These difficult slopes offer an exciting potential for high-altitude side treks to a number of passes around 17,000 ft. which lead into spectacular mountain valleys and glacier basins both east and west of the Thak Khola canyon. Of these high routes, the least difficult and most popular one is the climb to Meso Kanto pass (16,830') east of Jomsom. This pass opens eastward into the glaciated Tilichho Lake basin and other more remote high valleys to the north.

The mountain views from Meso Kanto are superb, and in addition to the eastward descent to Tilichho Lake, a route leads north from Meso Kanto to another pass and a series of peaks below 20,000 ft. on the headwaters of the Panda Khola; they can be climbed in good weather conditions for some of the most striking views in the Himalayas.

In snow-free conditions, the pass can be reached without technical climbing skill or equipment. The greatest danger on this route is from altitude sickness; a period for acclimatization should be scheduled between Jomsom and the top to make the climb both safe and enjoyable.

The route described below approaches Meso Kanto pass along the crest of a high ridge on the north side of the Longpoghyun Khola canyon, reaching an altitude of 17,500 ft. before descending to Meso Kanto from the northeast. A number of other trails which are more direct but harder to follow can be taken from Thini, the most southerly one keeps to the floor of the canyon and approaches the pass directly from the west. Its main disadvantage lies in having to climb on ice near the top. In addition, in keeping to the bottom of the canyon, good views of the surrounding terrain are missed.

*Jharkot Village in its romantic setting, perched on the edge of
Jhong Khola Canyon.* *(Photo P. Morris)*

*The small pagoda
temple at Muktinath.
Jwala Mai, the temple
of the miraculous five.
(Photo P. Morris)*

Timing and Equipment

During December, January and February, the intense cold and frequently heavy snowfalls are likely to make it impossible to reach Meso Kanto pass. The most favourable conditions are found during October, November, April and May. In early fall and late spring, Meso Kanto may be entirely free of snow for a few weeks.

Although the pass can be reached in a strenuous day-hike from the hut at Nama Phu pastures, in order to reach Tilichho later or to explore the area north of Meso Kanto, a tent, stove and food must be carried. Cold weather and snow must be expected at the altitude of the pass, and clothing and bedding should be expedition quality for a camp at the top.

The trail to Meso Kanto Pass and Tilichho Lake climbs up the canyon of the Longpoghyun Khola onto the north shoulder of Tilichho Peak. In the winter, ice and snow may be encountered at Thini before the climb is even begun.

52

Jomsom (8,900') to Nama Phu (13,400'): 6 hours
Proceed down the east bank trail from Jomsom to Thini (see page 40). Take the steep trail which ascends directly east from Thini to a notch on the main ridge running east from Jomsom to form the north wall of the canyon on the Longpoghyun Khola. From the notch, the trail climbs more gradually along the south side of the ridge, reaching a group of yak herders' huts about an hour beyond the village; a second group is reached an hour beyond the first.

The trail climbs diagonally up through the brush and low alpine vegetation above here, rising and falling along the north canyon wall, and it eventually crosses two tributary creeks. Beyond the creeks, the trail turns south briefly and climbs steeply up a grassy ridge to a large open grazing ground called **Nama Phu.** A good campsite with water is found at the upper end of this meadow, about 5 hours from Thini. Mountains visible from Nama Phu include Dhaulagiri, Tukche Peak, Tilichho Peak and the Nilgiris.

Nama Phu (13,400') to Meso Kanto (16,730'): 1 or 2 days
Beyond Nama Phu, the best approach to Meso Kanto is along the crest of the high ridge to the north which runs from Jomsom to Thinigaon Peak (18,500') just northeast of the pass. Turn northeast from Nama Phu, and climb to the crest of the main ridge. Follow the crest as it curves around toward the east, arriving at a saddle (17,500') under Thinigaon Peak. From here, turn southwest and descend to the pass along the west slopes of the peak. Reach **Meso Kanto Pass** in about 4 hours from Nama Phu.

A rocky track leads down to the east from the pass, staying on the south side of the valley but passing below the foot of Tilichho glacier to **Tilichho Lake** (16,140'). In bad weather or in the presence of symptoms of altitude sickness, it can be dangerous to make the descent to the lake.

From the 17,500-ft. pass north of Thinigaon Peak, it is possible to descend eastwards to a campsite in the headwaters of the Panda Khola at 15,500-ft. From this point, it is possible to continue northeastward, climbing to a pass at 19,000 ft. on the north shoulder of a peak at 20,505 ft. about halfway between Meso Kanto and the Thorong La east of Muktinath. Views of Annapurna and the Mountains of Mustang from here are unexcelled.

The Dhaulagiri Icefall

Between the summits of Dhaulagiri and Tukche Peak, the massive Dhaulagiri hangs suspended over the valley floor west of Larjung. At the foot of the icefall, a number of yak huts and a good campsite are found in pastures above 12,000 ft. This area can be reached without difficulty in one day from the Thak Khola, and the mountain views here, especially of the Annapurna summits, are superb.

The icefall was explored by the pioneering French expedition of 1950 as a possible route onto the upper slopes of Dhaulagiri, but the route proved extremely dangerous, and it was abandoned; in the spring of 1969, an avalanche on the icefall killed seven members of an American Dhaulagiri expedition.

About 15 minutes south of Larjung, the small settlement of Ghattekhola is located on the bank of a stream, the Ghatte Khola. Its headquarters are north and east of the Dhaulagiri icefall, and a trail climbs west from Ghattekhola along the south side of the stream. Passing the small village of **Nauri** soon after beginning the climb, continue up to open pastures under the cliffs just east of the foot of the icefall at 12,400 ft.

From this place, White Peak (17,262'), on the south-east ridge of Dhaulagiri directly south of the icefall, is very near and can be climbed in one day in favourable weather conditions. A day or more may be spent exploring along the base of the steep slopes between White Peak and the east ridge of Tukche Peak (22,703').

The Modi Khola and
The Annapurna Sanctuary

The principal peaks of the western portion of the great Annapurna Himal, including Hiunchuli, Annapurna South, Fang, Annapurna, Ganagapurna, Annapurna III and Machhapuchhare, are arranged almost precisely in a circle about 10 miles in diameter with a deep glacier-covered amphitheatre at the centre. From this glacier basin, known as the Annapurna Sanctuary, the Modi Khola knifes its way south in a narrow gorge fully 12,000 ft. deep. Further south, the gorge opens up into a wide and fertile valley, the domain of the Gurungs. The middle and upper portions of Modi Khola offer some of the best short trekking routes in Nepal, and the valley is located so that these treks can be easily combined with treks into the Kali Gandaki region to the west.

The Sanctuary provided the setting for one of the most exciting climbs in mountaineering history, the ascent of the South Face of Annapurna by a British expedition in 1970. The south Face is a giant, nearly vertical ice wall rising over two miles straight up out of the sanctuary. The 1970 group, led by Chris Bonnington, employed complicated ice-climbing techniques at great altitude in the most technically demanding ascent ever made on an 8,000-meter peak. In spite of the great heights of the surrounding peaks and ice walls, the valley floor between 12,000 and 14,000 ft. can provide comfortable camping spots in good weather.

Timing

From December to March, the Sanctuary is covered with a blanket of snow, obscuring the trails and making the footing difficult — and in this deep basin, the cold can be very intense. In April and May however, the weather is much warmer, and for a few weeks before the monsoon's arrival in June, the snows recede and leave the flowering meadows exposed. Although clouds from early in the day in spring, obscuring the mountain scenery, groups desiring to camp in the Sanctuary should choose April or May for the trek. For those who wish to use available shelter along the way and make a day hike into the Sanctuary, returning to Hinko cave the same day, the clearer but colder months of early fall undoubtedly offer the best conditions for the trip.

There are now three lodges near Machapuchare Base Camp, so it is no longer strictly necessary to stay at Hinko Cave for trips to the Annapurna Sanctuary. The lodges are not Hiltons, but they do serve to give primary shelter.

Recently - 1986 - quite good food has been available at Hinko Cave. If this service has been maintained, it will no longer be necessary to carry 4 days supply of food to the Base Camp.

Since the entrance to the Sanctuary lies two days' walk above the last occupied settlements, it is necessary to come equipped with food and other supplies. The simplest trek, a day hike into the Sanctuary from Hinko Cave and back, can be made with only four days supply of food and without a stove. To camp in the Sanctuary, however, a stove and a tent are almost a requirement. Tinned food such as cheese, porridge, milk, fruit and sardines, as well as local foods, can be purchased in Birethanti and sometimes in Chandrakot or Ghadrung.

Corrections to this guide

Spare a tear — or at least a thought — for a publisher in London who is trying to help trekkers in the field in Nepal. You may like to help us keep this guide up to date, by passing precise information on changed circumstances suitable for incorporation in the next edition.

It is firmly within the best traditions of the mountain code to do what you can to help those coming after you — whether it be to ensure that there is a supply of fuel on hand in a hut or to report on changes that have taken place which could affect the planning of treks.

Rest assured that your letters will be received with gratitude and examined with care.

We do ask however that information sent be **precise**. Please don't use phrases like "a bit further along the track" but say "about a quarter of a mile further along the track, on the left hand/northern side..."

Don't write simply of a lodge, but give a note as to its location and appearance, e.g. "About a hundred yards past the bridge and set some 50 yards back from the north side of the track, is a two storied stone lodge with accommodation for up to 20 persons." Think of the sort of information you might want yourself. Help us to give it.

The Annapurna Sanctuary can be approached from Pokhara by at least three different routes; all of them come together at the village of Ghadrung on the west wall of the Modi Khola canyon.

1.   Pokhara-Chandrakot-Sholebhati-Ghadrung:
2 days, 13½ hours.
Proceed to Chandrakot by the route described for the initial stages of the Jomsom trek. Instead of descending into the Modi Khola canyon to Birethanti, turn north near the western edge of town, and follow the wide trail which angles gently downhill to the right past the school. The trail remains high on the canyon wall for about an hour between the Chandrakot and the village of **Phatlikhet** where it turns then heads steeply downhill to the bottom of the canyon. One hour beyond Phatlikhet, cross the Modi Khola on a temporary wooden bridge to a number of tea shops and hotels on the west side called **Sholebhati.** During late spring, snow runoff may wash the Sholebhati bridge away, making the crossing here impossible. Inquire at Chandrakot about the condition of the bridge before starting this way. From Sholebhati, follow the trail upstream on the west bank, starting to climb about 20 minutes beyond the bridge; much of the trail consists of wide stone steps. Climb through the village of **Kimche** (5,400') and reach **Ghadrung** (6,800') about 2½ hours beyond Sholebhati. The first two buildings in this large and well-ordered Gurung village are hotels.

2.   Pokhara-Chandrakot-Birenthanti-Ghadrung:
2 days, 14½ hours
When the bridge at Sholebhati is out, descend to Birenthanti, and cross the big suspension bridge there. From the west end of Chandrakot, take the trail which descends steeply west below the viewpoint, and in 1½ hours, cross the big bridge into **Birethanti.** The trail up the west bank from here leaves the village between the suspension bridge and the Gauchan Lodge, the first building on the right. It is difficult to follow through the cultivated terraces at first, but it becomes a well-defined trail on a slightly higher ground behind the hotel. Follow it upstream near the hillside; it stays low and does not climb. In 1½ hours or a little less, rejoin the first route at Sholebhati. Proceed upstream to **Ghadrung** in 2½ more hours.

3. Pokhara-Dhampus-Landrung-Ghandrung:
2 days, 12½ hours.

The most direct route to Ghadrung bypasses Kaski Danda entirely and climbs north from Suikhet to reach an altitude of 7,100 ft., considerably higher than the lower southern routes. Proceed from Pokhara to **Suikhet** according to the description of the first day of the Jomsom trek, and follow the trail which climbs the north wall of the Yangdi Khola canyon.

Reach the village of **Astam** (4,600′) in 1 hour at the top of the ridge above Suikhet. From here, the trail continues to climb westward, staying near the crest of the ridge to Hyengjakot, a few minutes beyond Astam. The ruins of a medieval fortress which once commanded a small feudal kingdom are located here, and views down both sides of the ridge are impressive.

Dhampus (5,800′) is reached in another hour of fairly level trekking; it will take about 5 more hours to reach Langdrung from Dhampus. The trail goes over a 7,100-ft. pass about 2½ hours beyond here, then it descends to **Landrung** (5,800′) on the east canyon wall opposite Ghandrung. Now descend about 1,000 ft. to the Modi Khola, cross on a wooden bridge, and climb steeply up the other side to the village of **Ghandrung** after 2½ hours from Landrung.

Ghandrung, pronounced "Ghandruk" by residents, is one of the largest Gurung villages in Nepal, and it is typical in many respects. Its orderly rows of neat slate-roofed houses are clustered on the canyon wall amid a complicated network of terraces where wheat and barley are grown. The ridge above the village is a flyaway for eagles, hawks and vultures, and these enormous birds often circle in, right above the rooftops, to gain altitude in the afternoon thermals. The shops in the southern end of the village offer accommodation and a small selection of tinned foods.

Ghandrung (6,800') to Chhumro (6,500'): 5 hours

Climb through the village on a wide stone trail leading to a small creek canyon north of town. Cross the creek, and begin a gradual ascent to a notch at 7,300 ft. at the summit of a ridge dividing this creek from the Kymna Khola. The notch, with a tea shop at the top, is 1½ hours beyond Ghandrung. Now descend to the Kyumnu Khola, angling west and away from the Modi Khola to reach some tea shops at a bridge (5,800') an hour below the notch. Cross the creek, and climb directly up the other side on a steep dirt path to an elevation just below that of the notch south of the Kyumnu Khola.

After gaining back the lost elevation, the trail turns back toward the east on the contour and heads back out into the main river canyon. Rounding the corner of the ridge and turning back up the Modi Khola again, the trail makes a steep descent into the village of **Chhumro,** reached in 2½ hours from the Kyumna Khola bridge. There is a bamboo hut operating as a hotel in the south end of the village, but better accommodations can be found in a two-story house just uphill to the left of the hut.

Latterly, two lodges (International Hotel and Orchid Lodge) have been opened. These have reportedly offered excellent food and a really hot shower.

Chhumro (6,500') to Kuldi Ghar (7,800'): 3¾ hours

The trail goes downhill through the village, staying to the left of the small knoll on the near side of the Chhumro Khola. Descend into the canyon, cross the river, and climb steeply up the other side a short way, following the trail as it angles back out into the main river canyon. On the shoulder of the ridge around which the main canyon is re-entered, there is a viewpoint about an hour beyond Chhumro. From here, the village of Kuldi, the last village in the canyon, is visible upstream and below the trail. Now the trail angles gradually upward to the north along the west wall of the main canyon and passes above the village of **Kuldi.** About 3½ hours after leaving Chhumro, a single stone hut called **Kuldi Ghar** is located in a clearing; it lies just beyond a place where the trail crosses a steep patch of exposed bedrock on which crude footholds have been cut.

If Kuldi Ghar is reached later than afternoon, consider staying overnight and continuing to Hinko Cave the following day. It will take between 5 or 6 hours to reach the cave, and in snowy weather, it may take longer; the trail can be difficult to follow near Hinko after snowfall.

Kuldi Ghar (7,800') to Hinko Cave (10,000'): 5¾ hours

The trail descends from the hut and soon becomes a level stone pathway leading to the Kuldi Experimental Sheep Farm, a British aid project. The way is marked here with two signs, and beyond the farm, the trail drops steeply into the ravine of a tributary creek then climbs up the other side, angling back out into the main canyon. Now resume the gradual climb through heavy bamboo and rhododendron forests, dropping into tributary ravines occasionally, but generally maintaining a steady uphill grade. Through this stretch, the trail is often wet and muddy from groundwater seepage and melting snow.

After 2½ hours from Kuldi Ghar, as the trail nears the mouth of the narrow Modi Khola gorge it passes through an open grazing ground called **Tomo** (8,400'), a good place to camp. About half an hour further on, the trail descends and approaches the river at a place where a number of waterfalls are spread out in thin sheets on the mossy cliffs across the river. Hinko is about 2½ hours beyond and 2,700 ft. higher than this place. The trail continues climbing steadily through dense forests, becoming muddier and harder to negotiate. Finally, the trail exits from the underbrush onto the bank of a boulder-strewn creek bed; across the creek and uphill to the left, a giant overhanging boulder forms **Hinko Cave.** Scramble down the bank, and follow the creek-bed upstream until parallel with the rock before climbing up the other side to the cave.

Hinko Cave (10,000') to Annapurna Base Camp (13,900'): 7½ hours

A few minutes beyond Hinko, the trail disappears into a rocky stream bed, but stone cairns mark the trail slightly downhill on the opposite side. From here on, the trail is broken and very indistinct, often disappearing into landslides and creek-beds without a trace other than cairns. Another gully lies just beyond the first; ascend on the far side into bamboo and scrub. The trail eventually leads down to the bank of the river and travels along the water's edge a short way, approaching the turn into the Sanctuary. Three to four hours beyond Hinko, an old moraine ridge seems to split the canyon, with the river in a deep ravine on the right, and a small draw leading to the Sanctuary on the left. This is the site of the 1957 British Machhapuchhare base camp (12,000'), and there are two routes which may be taken into the Sanctuary from here.

The easier way is to stand under the moraine ridge, keeping to its left and following the little draw near the canyon wall. It swings around into the Sanctuary and climbs steadily, parallel to the moraine ridge. After 1½ hours, reach a tributary moraine blocking the upper end of the draw, and climb up to the right onto the main lateral moraine ridge. From there, the view of the Annapurna South face is tremendous. This place can also be reached by climbing directly up onto the moraine ridge at its foot from Machhapuchhare base camp and following its crest as it swings around into the Sanctuary. This way requires more time, but good views of the Sanctuary appear earlier on the higher route.

The Annapurna base camp is 1½ to 2 hours beyond the junction of the moraines. Climb down the west slope of the moraine, and go out onto the glacier which is fairly level and safe. The base camp is located on a shelf near the west side of the glacier at the foot of a spur from Annapurna South.

The most comfortable camp sites in the Sanctuary are in the meadows near the Machhapuchhare base camp at the foot of the moraine ridge. From here, day hikes can be made toward the Annapurna base camp and to other parts of the basin. Tent Peak and Glacier Dome, on the north side of the Sanctuary, can be reached by climbing down into the steep ravine under the foot of the main glacier and up the other side. Many days may be spent in pleasant exploration of this fascinating basin. Avalanches are common in the Sanctuary, however, even down as far as Hinko cave. Keep to higher grounds when possible, and pay attention to avalanche tracks and debris when choosing a campsite.

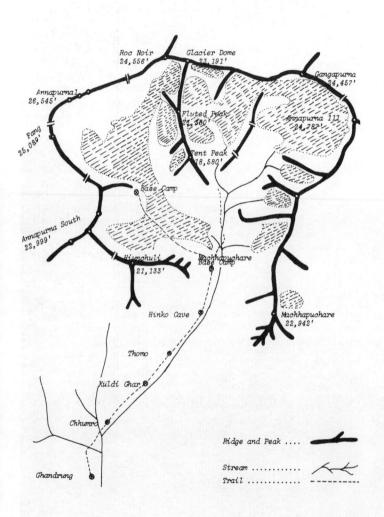

Roc Noir
24,556'

Glacier Dome
23,191'

Gangapurna
24,457'

Annapurna I
26,545'

Fang
25,089'

Fluted Peak
21,580'

Annapurna III
24,787'

Tent Peak
18,580'

Base Camp

Annapurna South
22,999'

Himchuli
21,133'

Machhapuchare
Base Camp

Hinko Cave

Machhapuchare
22,942'

Thomo

Kuldi Ghar

Chhomro

Ghandrung

Ridge and Peak ....

Stream ....

Trail ....

Annapurna glacier and Bonnington's Base Camp area —
Sanctuary.

Japanese Trekkers an Annapurna Base Camp area — Sanctuary.

The beginnings of the Modi Khola.

Annapurna South and Fang from the Sanctuary

Machhapuchhare from the Sanctuary.

Ghorapani—Ghandrung Connection

The Jomsom and Annapurna Sanctuary treks are connected by a system of trails leading from Ghorapani pass over a shoulder of Annapurna South to Ghadrung in the Modi Khola canyon, making it possible to complete both treks with a minimum of back-tracking. Apart from the convenience of this route, the spectacular view from the summit of the ridge (10,000'), which is covered with dense rhododendron forests and scattered alpine pastures, makes it one of the most beautiful stretches in the entire area. In combination with the trek to Ghorapani — the first three stages of the Jomsom trek — and one of the three Pokhara-Ghandrung routes, the connection forms a circuit which can be completed in as little as six days. This circuit is probably the best short trek from Pokhara, ideal for those who do not have time to visit Jomsom or the Annapurna Sanctuary,

The Ghorapani-Ghandrung section has a reputation of being difficult to follow, and since the many branching paths on top of the ridge are sometimes small and confusing, and because of a complicated junction at the top of the ridge, it is recommended the crossing not be attempted without a compass and a good map showing contour lines. Those with little trekking experience should hire a local guide at either Ghorapani or Ghandrung to take them across. Because of the difference in elevation between Ghorapani and Ghandrung, the crossing is easier going east, and it can be made that way in 8 hours.

Ghorapani (9,300') to Thante (8,600'): 4 hours
The trail to Ghandrung starts from Ghorapani Pass and climbs directly eastward up the broad crest of the main ridge which separates the Kali Gandaki and the Modi Khola valleys. The lower part of the ridge is covered with dense forests; higher up the trail passes through scattered meadows where the view of Dhaulagiri is unobstructed. After a climb of 2 hours from Ghorapani pass, descend slightly into a saddle at the first pass, marked by a prayer flag at 10,000 ft.

At this point, the trail from Chitre, wider and more prominent than the Ghorapani trail, comes up the draw on the left to join the Ghorapani trail in the saddle. Make an abrupt turn to the right at the pass, and descend through a broad meadow, keeping close to a depression in its centre which soon becomes a shallow draw, then a creek. The draw eventually opens up into the canyon of the Bhurungdi Khola, and the trail winds down along the creek over slipper rocks beside tumultous waterfalls. The upper part of this steep ravine is the most difficult stretch on the Ghorapani-Ghandrung crossing; progress will be particularly slow in conditions of ice and snow.

Further downstream, the ravine becomes a deep rocky gorge, and the trail parallels the creek through dense forests. After a descent of about 2 hours, reach a single stone hut called **Thante** in an open spot beside the creek. It is a perfect place to spend the night. Three lodge/restaurants have opened here recently.

Thante (8,600′) to Ghandrung (6,800′): 4 hours
Just beyond the hut, the trail crosses to the east bank of the stream and climbs up the bank into the forest, leaving the Bhurungdi Khola for good. Angling uphill around the ridge, cross a shoulder about 300 ft. above Thanté, and begin the descent into another creek ravine. Crossing this second creek, climb about 500 ft. out the far side to the last pass at 9,000 ft., marked with a rectangular **Chautara**, a stone resting bench about 1½ hours beyond Thante; from here, Ghandrung can be reached in 2½ hours.

Beyond this pass, resist the temptation to descend slightly northeast on one of the many cow trails in the forest; they all lead down into the Kyumnu Khola. The correct trail goes southeast, descending toward the right and angling around the front of a narrow spur. Reach a large clearing with another rectangular **chautara** about 20 minutes below the pass. Beyond here, the trail descends steeply into the canyon of a creek which flows toward Ghandrung. Reach a clearing about 1½ hours below the pass from which the upper houses of Ghandrung are visible. Continue to descend to the bottom of the canyon, cross the creek, and follow it downstream through rubble and boulders along the south side of the wide ravine. Reach the main Ghandrung—Chhumro trail shortly, and turn right to the first houses of **Ghandrung.**

Dumre via Manang and the
Thorong Pass to Jomsom

Manang, the region north of the Annapurna Himal, was opened
to trekkers in 1977. This region of Tibetan influence is not only
culturally interesting, but also provides some fine mountain views.
The view from Manang village itself, at 11,600', is most dramatic,
with views of the Annapurnas and a huge icefall tumbling into a
lake below the village.

Manang is most easily reached from Dumre on the Kathmandu-
Pokhara road. A trip up the Marsyandi to Manang can be varied
on the return by following the trail back to Tarkughat and then
walking west to Pokhara. A complete circuit of the Annapurna
Himal may be made by crossing the Thorong La pass, a 17,490'
pass between Manang and Muktinath, then following the Kali
Ghandaki route back to Pokhara.

The Thorong La should be crossed only from east to west
(Manang to Muktinath), and not used as an approach to Manang
from the Kali Ghandaki. It is a climb of more than 5,000' from
Muktinath at 12,460' to the top of the pass, and there is not a
single suitable place to camp during this entire climb. Most
unacclimatized trekkers will find this ascent impossible, and it is
certainly unsafe to spend a night in the open along this route.
Travelling from Manang to Muktinath, there is a suitable camping
place halfway up the climb, making it both possible and safe in
this direction.

There is an alternate route between the Kali Ghandaki and safe
and easy Manang via Tilichho Lake. But this trail is very hard to
follow, and in many places simply disappears. This route is not
recommended except as a side trip from Jomsom as described on
page 42.

Timing

A trek to Manang village can be made at any time of the year. The period from October to November provides the clearest skies and the best mountain views, but the local Manang people use the trail from Dumre to Manang year-round, so there is never a problem with the trail. If you plan to cross Thorong La pass, you should schedule the trek in October or early November, or else wait until April or May. The pass is often snowbound during the winter months.

The trek from Dumre to Manang, over Thorong La to Muktinath, and down the Kali Ghandaki to Pokhara can be made in as few as 20 days. It is best to allow longer for acclimatization in Manang before crossing the pass, for extra time in case of delays caused by snow on Thorong La, and for exploration of villages in both Manang and the Kali Ghandaki Valley. 25 or 30 days is not too much for this trek.

Equipment

There are a few small hotels and bhatis along this route, and in Manang itself it is possible to sleep in many of the houses in the village. But for a crossing of Thorong La a tent is an important item, because the crossing requires 2 days and there is no shelter en route.

Otherwise, the equipment suggested in the preceding sections is sufficient. The Manang route was opened to trekkers only in 1977, so that facilities are still very much geared to local people. If you want tinned food or anything not in the local diet you should carry it yourself.

Kathmandu (4,360') to Dumre (1,180') 5 hours

From Kathmandu, take a bus to Dumre, just past Mugling (890')
where the Trisuli and Marsyandi rivers join to form the Narayani.
Most buses stop to enable passengers to have lunch at Mugling.
The express minibus is much faster, and not much more expensive
than taking a local bus. On the express bus you have to pay for
the whole trip to Pokhara and then get off at Dumre. Dumre is
at the beginning of the new road being constructed up the
Marsyandi Valley to Besi Sahar, and the first 2½ days of the trek
at along this hot dusty road.

Dumre (1,180') to Turtore (2,400') 4 hours

Do not spend the night at Dumre. Begin walking immediately north
up the Marsyandi valley, crossing a small river on a set of stones,
and passing through paddies and small villages. Much of the time
the trail follows the motor road, but it sometimes gets off the road
into the shade of a few sal trees. Make a gradual climb to the
Gurung bazaar of **Bansar** (1,600'), where you can spend the night
if you took a late bus from Kathmandu. The trail continues to climb
to the top of a ridge that overlooks the whole Marsyandi Valley.
You can see the thousands of rice paddies that fill this fertile region.

Make a steep descent to the west bank of the Marsyandi. Follow
the river north along its west bank through a number of tiny villages
and past many large pipal and banyan trees offering shady resting
places along this hot section of the route. Make a short climb to
Chambas (2,300') on a low ridge above the river. If it is clear,
there are good views from here of Baudha Himal (21,890') and
Himal Chuli (25,897'). From Chambas, make a descent into a
saddle and climb up to the village of **Turtore** (2,400') where you
can find small hotels and restaurants serving both trekkers and
the construction workers for the new road.

Turtore (2,400') to Philesangu (2,100') 7 hours
Follow the trail downhill again to the Marsyandi river. There is a bridge here that leads to **Palangtar,** the airport serving Gorkha. Instead of crossing the bridge, stay on the west bank of the river and follow it north as the valley becomes a little steeper until you reach another large suspension bridge. Across this bridge is the village of **Takughat** (1,500'). If you are eating in bhatis, it would be best to cross the river here and eat in this well stocked bazaar.

To proceed to Manang do not cross the bridge, but continue to follow the trail and motor road up the west bank, descending to cross a large stream, then keep walking north up a straight and level stretch of road, through **Bhote Oralo** and on to **Philesangu** (2,100'), a Thakali bazaar situated just above the Marsyandi River where it rushes through a narrow tree-filled gorge. There is food and accommodation available in Philesangu.

Philesangu (2,100) to Kundi (2,600') 7 hours
Go back uphill a short distance to rejoin the motor road and continue north, climbing gradually and making many small ascents and descents as the road crosses small streams that flow into the Marsyandi. The road finally ends at **Besi Sahar** (2,600'), the administrative headquarters for the Lamjung district. There is the first of many police checkposts here.

Beyond Besi Sahar the trail narrows and makes a steep descent followed by an equally steep climb of 500 feet above the Marsyandi, which by now is flowing in a narrow wooded gorge. Beyond this climb, you must be careful when you cross several landslides that have washed away part of the trail. Keep climbing (but the trail is not steep) to the confluence of the Kundi and Marsyandi rivers, crossing over a rickety suspension bridge to the town of **Kundi** (2,600'). This is a large trading center and offers some interesting entertainment to anyone wishing to listen to the traders haggling over the cost of rice vs corn. You can sleep in this village or make a camp around the bend near the school.

Kundi (2,600') to Bondanda (3,950') 5½ hours

Leave the extensive town of Kundi and keep walking north along the Marsyandi until you come to a suspension bridge across the river at 3,200' elevation, near the village of Bhulbhulae. Here you cross to the east bank of the river and follow the trail up this side to avoid large cliffs that block the route on the west bank. There are good views of Peak 29 (24,654') and Himalchuli during the early part of this walk. Follow the trail as it climbs gently past a waterfall almost 200 feet high and through the small villages of Nandswara and Tarangje to the Nyadi Khola, a large stream flowing from the slopes of Manaslu. This river is crossed on another long, sagging suspension bridge. There are good places for bathing among the rocks below the bridge. From the bridge, make a short climb over a ridge and climb up through scrub forests to **Lampata** (3,900'), a village inhabited mostly by Tibetans, situated in a big horseshoe-shaped valley. There is some food and accommodation available here, but it is better to continue on for another half hour to the Chhetri village of **Bondanda,** on the top of the ridge at 3,950'. There is a shop, a tea house, and accommodation available at the far (north) end of the village.

Bondanda (3,950') to Chanje (4,500') 6 hours

From the shop at Bandanda, follow the trail down a large valley where rice is growing to the banks of the Marsyandi at 3,250 feet. There are 2 trail choices here. If there is an obvious trail across the Marsyandi, follow it across some gravel bars and temporary bamboo bridges and take an easy trail up the west bank of the river. This trail should be in operation during the dry season. By May the rains may have washed away the temporary bridges, so stay on the east bank, climbing over some ridges, to a suspension bridge over the Marsyandi at **Sange** (3,400'). Both routes join at this small village where tea or lunch may be had in one of about 3 possible bhatis.

Beyond Sange, follow the trail as it climbs high above the river on a trail cut into the near-vertical cliffs. There are few villages in this region because the soil is poor and the hillside is too steep for houses or cultivation. **Jagal** (4,200') is reached at the end of a long climb. There is some accommodation in this small village, and if you are staying in hotels, it is better to stay here than continue another 1½ hours to Chanje where the camping is good, but the hotels are poor.

From Jagal continue up the steep valley to **Chanje,** (4,500') a tiny village inhabited by Tibetans. Beyond the village the trail descends to the Marsyandi and crosses it on a wooden suspension bridge. About 10 minutes past the bridge is the best (and about the only) camping place along this stretch of trail.

Chanje (4,500') to Bagarchhap (7,100')
From Chanje the trail is not steep, except in a few places where it climbs high above the river to cross ridges. After about 2 hours walking in the steep narrow canyon, the Marsyandi valley suddenly widens into a broad flat-bottomed valley. This is the beginning of the Manang district, and the first village in the area is **Tal** (5,400') a village with many houses spread out among fields of wheat, corn, barley, buckwheat and potatoes, the staple crops of the Manang region.

Continue north to a large cement bridge, about 1½ hours beyond the first houses of Tal. Just beyond the bridge is Dharipani (6,100') where there are some bhatis and a police checkpost.

Continue north from Dharapani and immediately begin climbing. Soon, as you pass through deep forests, you will come to a trail leading off to the right. This trail descends to the river and climbs to Thongje, which can be seen across the Marsyandi. Continue on the main trail, staying on the lower trail, the new mule track, at every junction, and climb a short distance to **Bagarchhap** (7,100'). You are now in the Manang Valley itself, on the north side of the main Himalayan range of Annapurna and Lamjung Himal. To the east you can see Manaslu (26,760') at the bottom of the valley, and Lamjung Himal (22,921') and Annapurna II (26,041') may be seen through the trees to the south. From here the trail and the Marsyandi River turn west following the valley. There is an interesting **gompa** in Bagarchhap.

This compact village is typical of the Tibetan style construction that is found throughout the Manang valley. The stone houses are built closely together with flat roofs. There are a few fields near the houses, but most of the fields are situated outside the village. This arrangement of a village is very different from the rest of Nepal where each house is surrounded by extensive fields of rice, corn and wheat.

Bagarchhap (7,100') to Chame (8,900') 5 hours

Continue east from Bagarchhap up the tree-filled valley through a deep forest of pine and fir and climb to **Temang,** a small herder's settlement at 8,500 feet. Here you will often find Tibetans camped in tents, tending their herds of yaks and goats. There are people from the Nar-Phu valley to the north who move out of the cold regions into the warmer climate of the Manang Valley during the winter season.

From Temang, cross a stream and continue to climb in forests that look like those in the Western United States through **Charku** (8,800') and **Thangje** (8,700') to **Kuparkodo** (8,650'). This village also has a police checkpost to restrict travel up the Nar-phu Valley to the north. That entire valley is closed to foreigners.

Continue past the small clearing of Kuparkodo for another 40 minutes to Chame, the administrative headquarters for the Manang region. Here you will find a police checkpost, a bank, a wireless station and a few shops. There are a few bhatis where you can find reasonable accommodation. After you have settled in to your accommodation in Chame, follow the trail out of town, cross the bridge over the Marysandi, climb over the wall, and follow the river downstream about 50 yards. Here you will find 2 hot springs that will provide a super bathing place.

Chame (8,900') to Pisang (10,400') 6 hours

From Chame take the trail across the bridge, but turn left up the river, in the opposite direction from the hot springs. The trail now passes under some fantastic rock faces, some rising near-vertically out of the valley. Pass through the small village of Talung (9,150') and continue for another 1½ hours to a covered bridge across the Marsyandi. It is possible to get food and accommodation here at a large house on the left of the trail about 150 yards before you cross the Marsyandi River, however the accommodation is very limited.

Cross the bridge and make a short climb to **Bradan** (9,200'). There is no accommodation or food available here. After completing the formalities at Bradan, continue up the Marsyandi, crossing to the north bank, then re-crossing to the south bank on wooden bridges. Where the trail climbs up a small ridge, take the left-hand trail near some chortens and descend through forests to a bridge over the Marsyandi. Cross this bridge and climb to the village of **Pisang** (10,400'). You can probably find accommodation and food in one of the homes of this village. If you are camping, it is not necessary to cross the river and go into Pisang. There are excellent camping sites in the forests on the south bank of the river before you reach the bridge.

Pisang (10,400') to Manang (11,600') 4½ hours

From Pisang, descend and recross the river to rejoin the main trail up the south side of the Marsyandi. Climb several hundred feet up a ridge to a point that has a spectacular panoramic view of the upper Manang Valley. Here you can see the arid desert-like country that is typical from here to Jomsom. The big trees are left behind and the valley becomes very broad with views of many Himalayan peaks. The large peak at the head of the valley is Tukche Peak (22,705').

Descending steeply from the ridge, follow the trail through meadows where hers of sheep and goats are grazing. It is almost flat from here to Manang village. You will soon pass Ongde, the site for the Manang airport; its construction is well under way. Cross the Marsyandi a final time after the village of Gyang, and climb up to the picturesque village of **Bryagu** (11,300').

Most of this village of about 200 houses is hidden behind a ridge, so you have to go behind the ridge to see the village gompa and the Tibetan style houses. The gompa contains some of the oldest and best preserved paintings and statues in Manang. The villagers are quite proud that all pieces of religious art in their gompa are original treasures and that their statues and paintings were not sold as were many of the artifacts in gompas elsewhere in Nepal.

It is about a ¾-hour walk from Bryagu to **Manang** (11,600') along a trail that continually passes Tibetan Budhist chortens and mani walls as it makes its way through almost level desert-like country. Manang village is a large cluster of houses grouped very closely together with narrow passageways leading through the village. Accommodation may be secured in one of the local houses. The residences are all reached by ascending a log with steps notched in it; the ground floor of most houses is used as a stable. From Manang village there are excellent views of Gangapurna (24,455'), Annapurna III (24,788') and Glacier Dome (23,600') to the south.

Manang (11,600') to High Camp (14,500') 6½ hours

Spend at least one day in Manang village for acclimatisation before crossing the pass.

Climbing from Manang village itself, pass through upper Manang and then turn northwest up the Jarsang Khola valley. The trail is not steep here, but it climbs continuously past herder's huts. After about 4 hours you will come to a single stone house at 13,400'. There is a small spring that provides an adequate water supply just to the north, and a little bit downhill from his house. Continue climbing another 1½ hours. Here the trail descends steeply and crosses the Jarsang Khola on a wooden bridge. From the bridge, continue to ascend, now along the west bank of the stream, across a scree slope. The trail here is a little bit steep and unsafe because of the unstable rocks that it passes over. About an hour beyond the bridge you will reach a large meadow where the trail turns sharply west and starts a very steep climb uphill. This at 14,500' is the best campsite between Manang and the top of the pass. There is another possible campsite about 2½ hours higher, but there is no water at the campsite. It is best to camp at this spot for acclimatisation purposes rather than try to push on, over the pass.

High Camp (14,500') to Muktinath (12,460') 9 hours

Start the steep climb towards the pass as early as possible because it is a very long and tiring day. The trail is easy to follow when there is no snow because the local Manang people bring herds of yaks and sheep across this pass frequently. The climb starts steeply out of the Jarsang Khola Valley, then becomes a little more gentle as it winds its way among moraines and over ridges. The views along this route are excellent on a clear day, with Chulu Peak (21,618') to the east and Thorongtse to the north. There are also good views of the Annapurna Himal in the distance.

The Thorong La pass at 17,490' is reached after about 5 hours of walking from the camp. There is a small stream at about 16,500 feet that offers a possible lunch spot, but other than a small flat place at 16,000 feet, there is no spot big enough for a camp. There are many false summits, but the pass itself can be spotted in the distance marked by a large stone cairn and prayer flags. From the pass there are outstanding views in all directions, including a fine view of Dhaulagiri (26,796') across the Kali Ghandaki valley.

It is a long, steep kneecracking descent from the pass to Muktinath at 12,460'. The route from Muktinath to Jomsom is described on page 49.

Conversion Table: Feet to Metres

100 ft. = 30.48 m.

1,000	305	8,000	2,438	15,000	4,572	22,000	6,705
1,200	366	8,200	2,499	15,200	4,633	22,200	6,766
1,400	427	8,400	2,560	15,400	4,694	22,400	6,827
1,600	488	8,600	2,621	15,600	4,755	22,600	6,888
1,800	549	8,800	2,682	15,800	4,186	22,800	6,949
2,000	610	9,000	2,743	16,000	4,876	23,000	7,010
2,200	670	9,200	2,804	16,200	4,937	23,200	7,071
2,400	731	9,400	2,865	16,400	4,998	23,400	7,132
2,600	792	9,600	2,926	16,600	5,059	23,600	7,193
2,800	853	9,800	2,987	16,800	5,120	23,800	7,254
3,000	914	10,000	3,048	17,000	5,181	24,000	7,315
3,200	975	10,200	3,109	17,200	5,242	24,200	7,376
3,400	1,036	10,400	3,170	17,400	5,303	24,400	7,437
3,600	1,097	10,400	3,231	17,600	5,364	24,600	7,498
3,800	1,158	10,800	3,292	17,800	5,425	24,800	7,559
4,000	1,219	11,000	3,353	18,000	5,486	25,000	7,620
4,200	1,280	11,200	3,413	18,200	5,547	25,200	7,681
4,400	1,341	11,400	3,475	18,400	5,608	25,400	7,742
4,600	1,402	11,600	3,536	18,600	5,669	25,600	7,803
4,800	1,463	11,800	3,597	18,800	5,730	25,800	7,864
5,000	1,524	12,000	3,657	19,000	5,791	26,000	7,924
5,200	1,585	12,200	3,718	19,200	5,852	26,200	7,985
5,400	1,646	12,400	3,779	19,400	5,913	26,400	8,046
5,600	1,707	12,600	3,840	19,600	5,974	26,600	8,107
5,800	1,768	12,800	3,901	19,800	6,035	26,800	8,168
6,000	1,829	13,000	3,962	20,000	6,096	27,000	8,229
6,200	1,890	13,200	4,023	20,200	6,157	27,200	8,290
6,400	1,951	13,400	4,084	20,400	6,218	27,400	8,351
6,600	2,012	13,600	4,145	20,600	6,279	27,600	8,412
6,800	2,073	13,800	4,206	20,800	6,340	27,800	8,473
7,000	2,133	14,000	4,267	21,000	6,400	28,000	8,534
7,200	2,194	14,200	4,328	21,200	6,461	28,200	8,595
7,400	2,255	14,400	4,389	21,400	6,522	28,400	8,656
7,600	2,316	14,600	4,450	21,600	6,583	28,600	8,717
7,800	2,377	14,800	4,511	21,800	6,644	28,800	8,778